The Green Sea Psalter

Volume 1

The Green Sea

PSALTER

VOLUME 1: THE FIRST DECADE

Douglas Wilson

**BLOG & MABLOG
PRESS AND TIRE CENTER**
MOSCOW, IDAHO

Published by
Blog & Mablog Press and Tire Center
Moscow, Idaho
www.dougwils.com

Douglas Wilson, *The Green Sea Psalter, Volume 1: The First Decade*
©2024 by Douglas Wilson.

Book design and ebook conversion by Valerie Anne Bost.
Music typesetting by Michael E. Owens, noteworthymusicservices.com.
Cover photo by Dave Hoefler on Unsplash.

All Scripture quotations are from the Authorized Version, public domain.
All music in this volume is in the public domain.

All rights reserved. No part of this publication may be reproduced, stored in a retrieval system, or transmitted in any form by any means, electronic, mechanical, photocopy, recording, or otherwise, without prior permission of the author, except as provided by USA copyright law.

Version: 20231024print

For Margaret Anita Dixon,
who arrived around the same time the edits for this book did.

Contents

Introduction to the Series *ix*

Psalm 1: Blessednesses *1*

Psalm 2: The Rod of Iron *9*

Psalm 3: From His Holy Hill *19*

Psalm 4: Faith Knows That God Hears *25*

Psalm 5: The Hatred of God *33*

Psalm 6: Transactions of Grace *43*

Psalm 7: No Level Playing Field *49*

Psalm 8: Under His Feet *57*

Psalm 9: Poetic Justice *65*

Psalm 10: Break Their Evil Arms *75*

Introduction to the Series

About twenty years ago, I began preaching through the book of Psalms, taking ten of them at a go. Each bundle of ten was a decade, and consequently I would be done with the meta-series when I had fifteen decades of psalms. That series was to be completed in 2024, so the year before, I began work on assembling for publication some various *psalmish* things I had done. The plan is to follow the pattern set by the various sermon series—ten at a time—for a fifteen-volume set.

The pattern followed with each psalm goes like this. It begins with the text of the psalm from the Authorized Version, centered and formatted without verse numbers or other notation. This is followed by commentary and observations on that psalm. Then the psalm in one (or two) metrical poems, followed by the musical notation of one of those poems for each psalm.

I hope this helps you uncover the wealth of spiritual riches contained in "God's hymnal."

PSALM 1

Blessednesses

Blessed is the man that walketh not in the counsel of the ungodly,
nor standeth in the way of sinners,
nor sitteth in the seat of the scornful.
But his delight is in the law of the Lord;
and in his law doth he meditate day and night.
And he shall be like a tree planted by the rivers of water,
that bringeth forth his fruit in his season;
his leaf also shall not wither;
and whatsoever he doeth shall prosper.

The ungodly are not so:
but are like the chaff which the wind driveth away.

Therefore the ungodly shall not stand in the judgment,
nor sinners in the congregation of the righteous.

For the LORD knoweth the way of the righteous:
but the way of the ungodly shall perish.

In many ways, this first psalm is a perfect preface to all of the other psalms. In the space of a few short verses, we have the entire compass of righteous and unrighteous living set before us. Not every possible word is spoken, but the fundamental issues of life are all here.

There is a great contrast here. The psalmist shows us that there are two, and only two, ways of living. The first kind of man is richly blessed, profoundly blessed. He is blessed all the way down. The phrase translated *blessed is the man* could literally be rendered "O the blessednesses of the man . . ." In this fallen world, the genuine happiness that is received under God's blessing is a live possibility, and it is set before us. God in His grace *offers* it to us (v. 1).

This blessed man is negatively described first. In the first place, this blessed man is one who does *not*. The beginning of blessedness is an understanding of the *antithesis*. Without such wisdom, without such an antithesis, everything gets blurred and smudged, and this includes the difference between happiness and wretchedness (v. 1).

We also see that sin progresses. We can identify a natural movement here—walk, stand, sit (v. 1)—compromise, dalliance, allegiance. The blessed man has no truck with the wisdom of fools;

he rejects the counsel of the ungodly. The concern here is with the teaching, the philosophy, the wisdom of those who do not walk with God. It does not end here, but it does begin here. The ungodly will say, "Look, *here* is true wisdom." Examples are not hard to find—pop-therapy psychobabble, scientism, or preachy sitcoms. Ungodly counsel, the way of sinners, and the seat of scoffers are *all* opposed to the law of God.

But the godly man does not just shun that which is wicked. That by itself would be an example of mere moralism. If we do not begin with the antithesis, we will belong soon enough to the devil's party. If we live by a truncated antithesis, merely shunning things that are "bad," we will soon find ourselves as Pharisees, belonging to . . . the devil's party.

The godly man knows how to find true delight. The law of God entrances him. He can't get over it. He reads it again and again. He meditates on it *constantly*—day and night. The word here for *meditates* is a word that comes from muttering, or mumbling. This man delights in the law of God to such an extent that we find him talking under his breath to himself about it (v. 2).

What is the result? He is like a tree planted by the waterside. Note first that *he is planted*. He did not do this for himself (v. 3). Since this is the case, his leaf does not wither, and his fruit is yielded in season. Now what is the nature of his fruit?

This passage says that it includes *whatever* he does (v. 3). The Bible teaches us that temporal prosperity is to be subordinated in our hearts and minds to spiritual prosperity, but the Bible does not set them necessarily at odds with each other. Consider what Paul teaches in 1 Timothy 4:8: "For bodily exercise profiteth little: but godliness is profitable unto all things." For the righteous man, as a general rule, *whatever* he does prospers.

And whatever the godly are, the ungodly are not. There are really only two ways to live. One way is to live as chaff. A tree is rooted and fruitful, but if we think about chaff, few things could be found that are more clearly and plainly rootless. Not only is this the case, but chaff is also worthless, and the wind drives it off (v. 4). Who wants it? It is blown away by the wind, and nobody wants to chase it.

It is a grave error to assume that the Old Testament saints knew nothing of the final judgment. Here the great congregation of all the saints is gathered by God (v. 5). The ungodly shall not stand there; they fall in the judgment. These are the ones who *stood* in the way of sinners, so they shall *not* stand in the judgment.

God knows the difference between wheat and chaff, which reveals the motive of many who want to deny the omniscience of God—whether practically or doctrinally. Like a toddler, they think if they cover their eyes, they can't be seen. God knows the way of the righteous, and we know from this that the way of the ungodly shall perish (v. 6).

What should we do? How should we walk? First, we should read all of the psalms, sing all of the psalms, mediate on the psalms, mutter under our breath about the psalms . . . with this antithesis in mind. Second, we must ditch the counsel of the wicked. We must not *listen* to these people. They reject the Word of God; what wisdom could they have? Third, we have to abandon ourselves to the Scriptures. Think of something, anything, that you truly delight in. How do you behave toward that thing? Now compare this with your approach to the Word. Fourth, we must seek blessedness. God prospers the work of those who fear Him. Seek *this* kind of prosperity, and accept no other kind. And fifth, remember the day of judgment. God knows and considers every step we take. He knows which road we are walking on. He will bring everything into judgment. We must remember and fear Him.

Blest is the man who does not walk
In ways of the ungodly man,
Who does not stand in paths of sin
And will not sit where mockers talk.

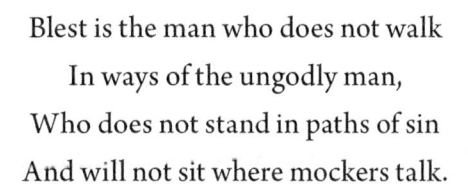

His full delight is in the law;
On holy laws he meditates.
All day and night he contemplates
And holds the truth in rev'rent awe.

Planted deep by the riverside,
This tree brings forth the season's fruit.
His leaf is nourished from the root;
Prosperity is full and wide.

Not so the wicked, who will die.
They are like chaff which blows away
And cannot stand on judgment day,
When He will lift the saints on high.

God knows the way of all His host,
The wicked die a godless death.
Praise Him, praise Him, those who have breath,
Praise Father, Son, and Holy Ghost.

Blessed is the man who does not walk
Where sinners stand, or mockers talk;
The law of God is his delight,
His meditations day and night.
By running streams his tree takes root
And bears in season godly fruit.
Not so the wicked! Their mocking laugh
Will dissipate like wind-blown chaff.
Under judgment, they will not stand
When fire comes down to cleanse the land.

Blest Is the Man Who Does Not Walk
Based on Psalm 1

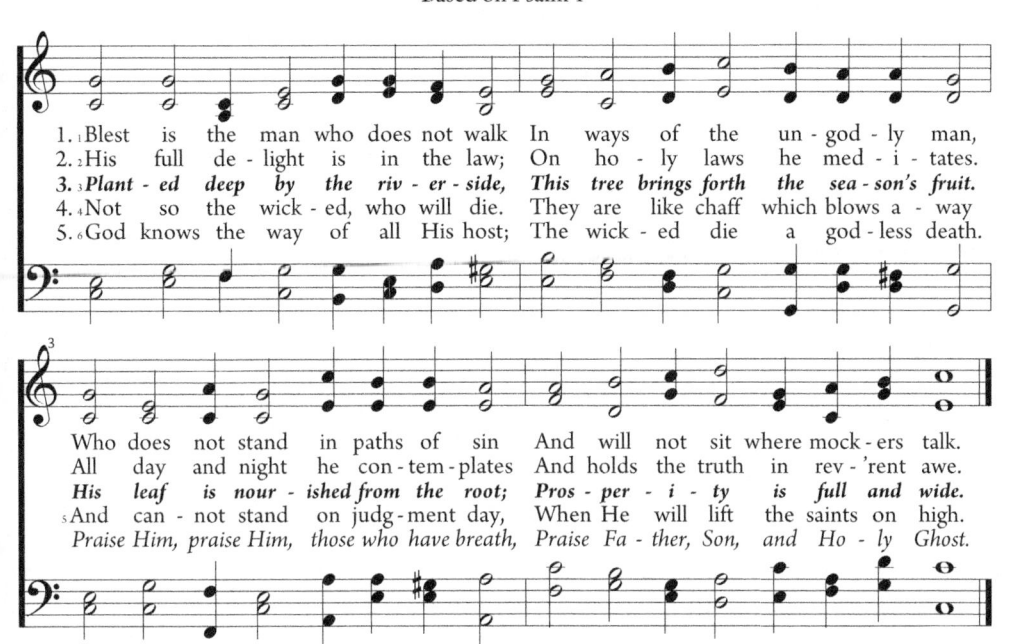

1. Blest is the man who does not walk In ways of the un-god-ly man,
2. His full de-light is in the law; On ho-ly laws he med-i-tates.
3. *Plant-ed deep by the riv-er-side, This tree brings forth the sea-son's fruit.*
4. Not so the wick-ed, who will die. They are like chaff which blows a-way
5. God knows the way of all His host; The wick-ed die a god-less death.

Who does not stand in paths of sin And will not sit where mock-ers talk.
All day and night he con-tem-plates And holds the truth in rev-'rent awe.
His leaf is nour-ished from the root; Pros-per-i-ty is full and wide.
And can-not stand on judg-ment day, When He will lift the saints on high.
Praise Him, praise Him, those who have breath, Praise Fa-ther, Son, and Ho-ly Ghost.

Music: Heinrich Schütz, 1661
Text: Douglas Wilson, 2000 ©

WER NICHT SITZT [BECKER 1]
8 8. 8 8.

PSALM 2

The Rod of Iron

Why do the heathen rage,
and the people imagine a vain thing?
The kings of the earth set themselves,
and the rulers take counsel together,
against the Lord, and against his anointed, saying,
Let us break their bands asunder,
and cast away their cords from us.
He that sitteth in the heavens shall laugh:
the Lord shall have them in derision.
Then shall he speak unto them in his wrath,
and vex them in his sore displeasure.
Yet have I set my king Upon my holy hill of Zion.

I will declare the decree: The Lord hath said unto me,
Thou art my Son; this day have I begotten thee.
Ask of me, And I shall give thee the heathen for thine inheritance,
and the uttermost parts of the earth for thy possession.
Thou shalt break them with a rod of iron;
thou shalt dash them in pieces like a potter's vessel.
Be wise now therefore, O ye kings:
be instructed, ye judges of the earth.
Serve the Lord with fear, and rejoice with trembling.
Kiss the Son, lest he be angry,
and ye perish from the way, when his wrath is kindled but a little.
Blessed are all they that put their trust in him.

In this psalm, we find a wonderful prophecy of the never-ending reign of Messiah the Prince.

The prophecy does not concern the reign of God in His sovereignty, which is the necessary result of the Creator's relationship to the world that He created, but rather a reign that results from His sovereign decree—the *mediatorial* reign of the Lord Jesus Christ. In other words, God rules the world as Creator and does so necessarily. But He rules the world *redemptively* through Jesus Christ.

We are Christians, and this means, among other things, that we should seek to have the New Testament teach us how to read the Old Testament. Our method for learning the meaning of this psalm should be to pay close attention to what the New Testament says about it. Any such New Testament references should be our anchor points.

Why do the heathen rage? We are told in Acts 4:24–28 that the first two verses of the second psalm are a prophecy of the *crucifixion*. We also learn of the Davidic authorship of the psalm there. If the New Testament says that David wrote it, then we know that David wrote it. In addition, we see the psalm is the basis for saying that the murder of Christ was a predestined event. God used the wickedness of men to save the world.

Moving on to the second anchor point, in Acts 13:33, we learn that verse 7 of our psalm is a prophecy of the *resurrection*: "God hath fulfilled the same unto us their children, in that he hath raised up Jesus again; as it is also written in the second psalm, Thou art my Son, this day have I begotten thee."

This verse is quoted in two other places also. Hebrews 1:5 shows us that this passage also depicts the supremacy of Christ over angels. And Hebrews 5:5 quotes it as describing Christ entering His office as high priest. Put them all together, and we see that in the resurrection, Christ is begotten from the dead, has entered into His high priestly work, and was made higher than the angels.

Then there is the reference to the rod of iron. The book of Revelation refers to verse 9 three times, and the usage there is very interesting. Revelation 19:15–16 refers to Christ's rule over the nations, with His wrath in view. Revelation 12:5 refers simply to Christ's rule over the nations. And Revelation 2:26–29 teaches us that Christ rules the nations through His saints. God has made us kings and priests on the earth.

What are the implications of all of this? This psalm has twelve verses. We know that verses 1–2 are about the crucifixion, that verse 7 is about the resurrection, and that verse 9 addresses the reign of Christ through His Word in the Church. What then do we learn from this about the rest of the psalm? Having established fixed points in the psalm (fixed by authoritative commentary from the New Testament), we are in a position to see what the rest of it means. The language of verse 3 refers to the nations' resentment over the fact that they had to plow underneath the yoke of the Lord Jesus Christ.

Then we come to the laughter of God. Consider two things. First, if the laughter of God can accomplish such great and terrible things, what will His wrath be like? And second, who would have thought of this—divine laughter!—when the sun was dark, the disciples scattered, our Lord in anguish, the Sanhedrin gloating, Satan triumphant, Peter wretched, Judas in despair, and Mary in tears?

And yet God will do what He has intended to do through all this. Despite His enemies' pitiful little schemes, the Lord will establish His King in Zion (v. 6), however little they might like it (v. 5).

Now, after the crucifixion and just after the resurrection, God Almighty extends an invitation to His Son, Jesus Christ—He invites Him *to just ask* (v. 8). What belongs to Jesus Christ now? What nation is not His present possession? Can you find one? Is there one He didn't want? Did He refuse to ask for one? Remember, the rod of iron extends over all of them (v. 9).

What therefore is the responsibility of our Congress, our Supreme Court, and our president? They must seek wisdom and receive instruction. They must serve God in their public civic capacity, with fear, joy, and trembling (v. 11). Remember that God's laughter overthrew all their impudent plans. Beware of His wrath (v. 12). This means, among other things, that the United States has the explicit duty to be a Christian nation.

When the church hears the Word of God rightly, the whole world is set to right. The three great offices of Christ are set before us in this psalm. He is the prophet—we must hear His words of instruction

(v. 10). He is king, established in Zion (v. 6). And He is priest (v. 7; Heb. 5:5).

We see that the Lord has already received His inheritance. The matter is settled. The question is not being brought before the United Nations for consideration. The reign of Christ has been established. The nations who object to this arrangement trouble the decrees of God about as much as dogs barking at the moon trouble the moon.

This is why Jesus Christ reigns redemptively throughout the entire earth. Christians are those who are called to believe what God has declared concerning this. The one who trusts His Word is always blessed. God has spoken on this glorious subject—are we blessed in hearing it? Do we believe Him? Jesus reigns from the river to the ends of the earth. Which river? It does not matter. From the Thames to the Hudson, from the Nile to the Ganges, from the Rhine to the Mississippi, from the Potomac to the Amazon, the name of the Lord will be praised, and pure sacrifices will be offered up to Him in every nation.

―

Why do the heathen nations vainly rage?
What prideful schemes are they in vain devising?
The kings of earth and rulers all engage
In evil plots, and in their sin contriving,
They take their stand against our GOD's Messiah;
They claim they will not keep His binding chains.
The One enthroned in highest heaven, higher,
Mocks them to scorn, on them derision rains.

He speaks to them in righteous, holy wrath;
God vexes them and shows His great displeasure.
"Yet so I set my King upon the path
That upward winds to Zion, My own treasure."
"'You are My Son, today You are begotten,'—
I will declare what God has said to Me—
'And not one tribe will ever be forgotten.
You will receive the world, just ask of Me.

"'The nations come; You are the only Heir,
The ends of earth will be Your own possession,
And, broken with a rod of iron there,
Rebellious pottery comes to destruction.'"
Now serve the Lord, with fear and gladness trembling,
And therefore, O ye kings, seek wisdom here.
How blessed are those who trust without dissembling,
Who kiss the Son and bow in reverent fear.

※

Why do the nations rage in vain?
Why do the peoples scheme?
The kings and rulers all disdain
The rule of God and dream
That they can break the hated chain
That represents Messiah's reign.

The One enthroned in Heaven roars
　　With laughter at the thought.
And then He turns and anger pours—
　　A sovereign lesson taught.
The King is crowned, all heaven adores
And sings before the palace doors.

I will proclaim the Lord's decree
　　And say, "You are my Son.
I am your Father, ask from Me
　　All lands beneath the sun.
Prepared your iron rod will be
To dash rebellious pottery."

So all you kings of earth, be wise
　　You rulers, be forewarned.
With fear submit and realize
　　That rebels will be scorned.
Now kiss the Son, do not despise—
In Him all blessed refuge lies.

Why Do the Heathen Nations Vainly Rage?
Based on Psalm 2

1. Why do the heath-en na-tions vain-ly rage? What pride-ful schemes are they in vain de-vis-ing? ₂The kings of earth and rul-ers all en-gage In e-vil plots, and, in their sin con-triv-ing, They take their stand a-gainst our GOD's Mes-si-ah; ₃They claim they will not keep His bind-ing chains. ₄The One en-throned in high-est Heav-en, high-er,

2. ₅He speaks to them in right-eous, ho-ly wrath; God vex-es them and shows His great dis-pleas-ure. ₆"Yet so I set My King up-on the path That up-ward winds to Zi-on, My own treas-ure. ₇'You are My Son, to-day You are be-got-ten,'— I will de-clare what God has said to Me— ₈'And not one tribe will ev-er be for-got-ten.

3. The na-tions come; You are the on-ly Heir, The ends of earth will be Your own pos-ses-sion, ₉And, bro-ken with a rod of i-ron there, Re-bel-lious pot-ter-y comes to de-struc-tion." ₁₁Now serve the LORD, with fear and glad-ness trem-bling, ₁₀And there-fore, O ye kings, seek wis-dom here. ₁₂How blest are those who trust with-out dis-sem-bling,

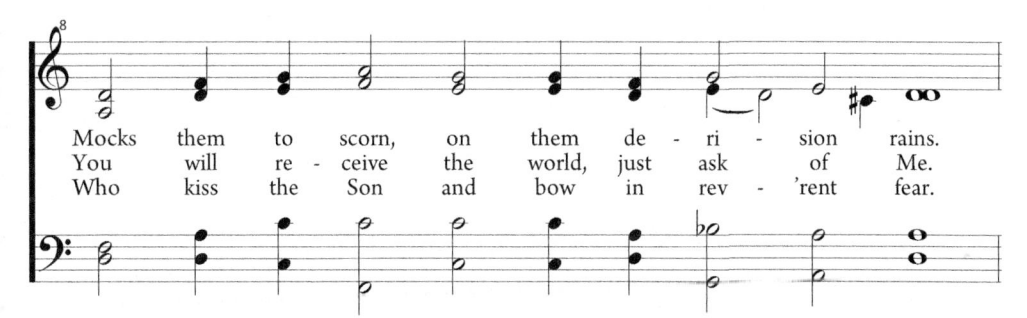

Mocks	them	to	scorn,	on	them	de-	ri-	sion	rains.
You	will	re-	ceive	the	world,	just	ask	of	Me.
Who	kiss	the	Son	and	bow	in	rev-	'rent	fear.

Music: *Genevan Psalter*, 1539; harm. Claude Goudimel, 1564
Text: Douglas Wilson, 2000 ©

POURQUOI FONT BRUIT [GENEVAN 2
10 11. 10 11. 11 10. 11 10

PSALM 3

From His Holy Hill

A Psalm of David, when he fled from Absalom his son.
Lord, how are they increased that trouble me!
Many are they that rise up against me.
Many there be which say of my soul,
There is no help for him in God. Selah.
But thou, O Lord, art a shield for me;
my glory, and the lifter up of mine head.
I cried unto the Lord with my voice,
and he heard me out of his holy hill. Selah.
I laid me down and slept;
I awaked; for the Lord sustained me.
I will not be afraid of ten thousands of people,

that have set themselves against me round about.
Arise, O Lord; save me, O my God:
for thou hast smitten all mine enemies upon the cheek bone;
thou hast broken the teeth of the ungodly.
Salvation belongeth unto the Lord:
thy blessing is upon thy people. Selah.

We are told in the book of Job that man is born to trouble as the sparks fly upward. In the third psalm, we discover what it means, in a time of such trouble, to find our rest and comfort in God alone. When David fled from Absalom, it was one of the greatest troubles of his life.

The context was this. Absalom, a wicked and ungrateful son, had successfully surprised his father with his revolt. At the same time, there were earlier causes much larger than Absalom's ingratitude. Although David had been forgiven for his sin with Bathsheba, there were long-term consequences nonetheless (2 Sam. 12:11–12).

David, despite a long and prosperous reign, had thousands of enemies within Israel. The night when David fled from Jerusalem, he had six hundred men with him. The counsel to Absalom that night was to send an army of twelve thousand after David. That counsel came from Ahithophel—Bathsheba's grandfather—and although the counsel was thwarted, it is still telling that an army of twelve thousand men was readily available.

Another significant detail is that David told the priests to keep the ark in Jerusalem. The Lord hears David's prayer in this psalm "out of his holy hill." Absalom thought he was in control of Jerusalem, but he was not.

This psalm is the first in which the Hebrew word *selah* occurs. It occurs only in poetry, and there has been much discussion over what it means. Many commentators hold that it indicates a pause in the singing to provide time for meditation or reflection. Others hold that it indicates a "lifting," either of volume, or perhaps of key. I take it as a required pause for meditation.

This psalm is David's cry to God. He may have written it after the crisis, when he was reflecting on it. But it is more likely, given the nature of the psalm, and the tone of it, that he composed this during his flight from his son. The psalm divides readily into four strophes.

"Many there be." The rebellion against David was centered in the ten northern tribes, those seduced by Absalom. The magnitude of the revolt was considerable. There were many who troubled David (v. 1). Their numbers troubled him, and so did their words. As Shimei cursed David in his flight, many said that God was done with David (v. 2). This shaft went home. David was an adulterer and a murderer. Did he deserve all this? In one way, yes. But was it true that there was no help for him in God? Absolutely not.

David still turned to God. God was a shield—a shield that completely surrounded him (v. 3). God was David's glory and, in his time of trouble, the lifter of his head (v. 3). They said to him that God would not hear. But David has not lost his voice (v. 4). God heard the prayer, and He heard it from His holy hill, Zion (v. 4).

And comfort comes. This is the peace that passes understanding. David laid down and slept soundly, not wracked by anxiety. He woke up, and the Lord had sustained him. Sleep is a manifest type of death. David was dead, but he faced it quietly, and woke in the morning (v. 5). David rested in the Word of God, and he will not be afraid, regardless of the numbers set against him. Nathan's prophecies had come true—one son had died, and another son had slept with his concubines.

But Nathan had said nothing about losing the throne. David therefore summons God to arise. God has been seated (v. 7), and David cries to Him: Rise up! God has broken the teeth of the wild animals who would devour David—they cannot do him any harm (v. 7). Salvation is from God; it truly is (v. 8). His blessing rests upon His people.

What applications might we draw? How are we to sing this psalm? What are we to learn?

You think you've got troubles? The Scriptures are given, in part, to comfort us in all our afflictions. Throughout the Word of God, we find more than enough examples to encourage us.

And we see here that only God can shield. Every self-protective device we might invent is a shield made out of two layers of tissue paper. Only God can shield us from the dangers of this world.

As David cried to the Lord, so may we. His arm is not too short to save. He hears the cries of His people. He knows your distress and wants you to cry out to Him from the midst of it. And it does not matter if Absalom controls the temple physically. The Lord can still answer out of His holy hill.

Therefore, we rest in the fact that salvation is the Lord's. We learn to pray when we learn who answers prayer, and who alone answers prayer. The answer to our prayers is not the result of a cooperative effort between us and God. We cry out, and He answers us from His holy hill. Our cry for help is not part of the answer—it is the prayer. Salvation is of the Lord, and of the Lord only.

O Lord, how many are my foes!
How many rise and dare oppose!
They laugh and mock and then propose
That God will not deliver me.

To them, my Lord, I do not yield.
My Glorious One remains my shield.
To you I cry, this prayer I wield.
You answer from Your holy hill.

I still lie down and go to sleep.
The Lord sustains, I do not weep.
Though enemies are thousands deep
And drawn up here on ev'ry side.

Arise, O Lord, deliver me!
With broken teeth the wicked flee.
From God, my God, comes victory
And blessing for His people here.

O Lord, How Many Are My Foes
Based on Psalm 3

1. O Lord, how many are my foes! How many rise and dare oppose!
2. They laugh and mock and then propose That God will not deliver me.

2. To them, my Lord, I do not yield. My Glorious One remains my shield. To You I cry, this prayer I wield. You answer from Your holy hill.

3. I still lie down and go to sleep. The Lord sustains, I do not weep. Though enemies are thousands deep And drawn up here on ev'ry side.

4. Arise, O Lord, deliver me! With broken teeth the wicked flee. From God, my God, comes victory And blessing for His people here.

Music: attr. Melchior Vulpius (1560–1616)
Text: Douglas Wilson, 2018 ©

DER TAG BRICHT AN
8 8. 8 8.

PSALM 4

Faith Knows That God Hears

To the chief Musician on Neginoth, A Psalm of David.
Hear me when I call, O God of my righteousness:
thou hast enlarged me when I was in distress;
have mercy upon me, and hear my prayer.
O ye sons of men, how long will ye turn my glory into shame?
How long will ye love vanity, and seek after leasing? Selah.
But know that the LORD hath set apart him that is godly for himself:
the Lord will hear when I call unto him.
Stand in awe, and sin not:
commune with your own heart upon your bed, and be still. Selah.
Offer the sacrifices of righteousness,
and put your trust in the LORD.

> There be many that say, Who will shew us any good?
> Lord, lift thou up the light of thy countenance upon us.
> Thou hast put gladness in my heart,
> more than in the time that their corn and their wine increased.
> I will both lay me down in peace, and sleep:
> for thou, Lord, only makest me dwell in safety.

*M*any believe that this fourth psalm was written on the same occasion as the one just before it—Absalom's revolt. Another strong contender for the context is during the time earlier in David's life when he was pursued by Saul. Whatever the specific situation was, the psalm was clearly composed during a time of great trouble and insecurity for David.

The heading gives the psalm to the chief musician. This shows the intent that, although it was written out of David's personal, individual experience, it was to be used in public, corporate worship. All of Israel was invited to make his experience their experience. And all of the Church is likewise invited to own David's experiences, viewing our own troubles in the light of his. The dedication to the chief musician also indicates the importance of musical leadership. The people were not to come to the temple and just wing it. The word *neginoth* refers, as we would put it, to the strings. The psalm has three sections—verse 1, verses 2–5, and verses 6–8.

What is the import of the first verse? This is David's cry to the Lord. God is called the "God of my righteousness." This gives us two precious truths. The first is that God is Himself righteous. The second is that God is *David's* righteousness as well. In this crisis, David depends upon what God has done in the past. Past deliverance is solid ground to stand on as you plead for present deliverance. The saint in trouble is encouraged by Scripture to say with importunity, *Hear me!*

Having addressed God, David takes an interesting turn here—he addresses his adversaries. "Sons of men" is a noble form of address. David combines an acknowledgment of their greatness with an acknowledgment of their folly (v. 2). The glory David refers to is his own honor and glory, the glory God had bestowed on him. He asks *how long* his foes will treat with contempt the one God has honored. Driven by envy, they will say anything. How long will they love vanity and chase down leasing (an old Saxon word meaning *falsehood*)?

We do not set ourselves apart. This is done for us and to us. Note that God sets the godly apart *for Himself* (v. 3). This being the case, *the Lord will hear.*

What is the central problem? Lack of reverence, a lack of a true fear of God, is what drives the sinful mind. This is particularly true when the sinful mind adopts a religious posture—when the hypocrite cops a pious pose. David's charge, therefore, is for his adversaries to "stand in awe" and to cease from their sin. They should think about their lives when they are on their beds. They should stop their sinful chatter and reflect. They should be *still* (v. 4). Paul quotes verse 4 in Ephesians 4:26 as "Be ye angry, and sin not." The word translated *stand in awe* means *to tremble* and can indicate trembling from either fear or anger, and the translators of the Septuagint went with the latter when they rendered it in Greek. Paul's use of it doesn't necessarily indicate his endorsement of the translation; rather, the phrase had probably entered common parlance, and he was simply repeating and confirming the sentiment as something true and correct.

David continues addressing the hypocrites: When they have reflected and consequently repented, then they should approach God with their sacrifices, trusting in Him (v. 5).

In the spirit of contentment, David returns to his prayer to the Lord. In doing this, he remembers the central folly of his adversaries—an autonomy that wants to manufacture its own standards and be its own god. They ask, "Who will show us good?" (v. 6), but their skepticism is just a thin excuse for their unbelief. The answer is found in the light of God's countenance. Although systematic theologies can describe God's goodness in the abstract, we can only *know* it when He shines on us with favor. Too often, analytic theologians want to talk about the God's characteristics as though they've got a schematic diagram of God and all His attributes drawn to scale. But how can you draw anything that's infinite to scale? Of course we can point—feebly—to the attributes of God as He's revealed them in Scripture, but the fundamental thing we must do is to define *good* as God showing favor to us. And if God looks down on His saints with pleasure, then sinners are madmen. In adverse circumstances, God's favor takes the form of His gift of contentment (v. 7). *God* puts gladness in our hearts. What kind of gladness is it? It is better than a glorious harvest. In this condition of glad trust, the saint can safely rest and sleep free of anxiety and turmoil even when enemies rage around him (v. 8). As Paul says in Philippians, it's a peace that passes understanding.

Again, David offers up his personal experience but does so in a way that enables the whole church to say *amen*. All believers throughout the history of the world can say, "This psalm is mine. David's troubles are my troubles, David's God is my God, David's salvation is my salvation, and David's gladness is my gladness."

So how do we appropriate this psalm? In the worship of the church, we address God, one another, and those not present. The worship of the church is not merely a religious meeting in a room; we are worshiping God in the heavenlies, and what happens in the world is a function of our doing so. Worship is warfare, a deadly instrument in the hand of God. He hears us and acts upon the words we speak to those who are not present to hear us, so they feel the tremors of what happens here. Worship in the heavenlies conquers the earth, not according to carnal weapons but by means of the proclamation of the truth.

But men in an unconverted condition love vanity, and they seek after falsehood. This includes many who grew up in the church. Lies are the currency of the devil, and those who deal in that currency are citizens of *his* kingdom. The lies are not represented as lies—they wouldn't work if they were. They are made to seem plausible. "Who will show us good?" can be made to appear a reasonable question.

There is, therefore, a necessary collision between the truth-tellers and the lie-tellers. If true worship is warfare, and if men in their sins are opposed to the good, then a comfortable compromise is not a possibility.

What is the fundamental issue here? There are two important applications. First, God *will* hear. When we offer God's word back to Him, as much of it as we can, He hears our prayers, and our songs. When we assimilate God's word, and, having assimilated it, we speak to Him, He hears us. Second, *faith knows that God hears*. This is why we can have an unearthly confidence. When everything around us appears hopeless, the trusting saint can lie down and sleep peacefully.

O Lord, please answer when I call!
O God, my strength and righteousness,
Your strength is great and mine is small—
Give me relief from my distress!

How long, O men, will you corrupt
My glory, turning it to shame?
How long will you with lies erupt
And serve the gods that have no name?

Know that the Lord has set apart
Unto Himself all godly men.
So, trembling, cease! And doubt, depart!
The Lord will hear my prayer. Amen!

So in your anger do not sin
When you lie down upon your bed.
Prepare your hearts and search within
Before the offered prayer is said.

While many scoff and many doubt
And say, "Who shows us any good?"
You fill us with more joy throughout
Our lives than grain or new wine could.

I will lie down and sleep in peace,
For You alone, O Lord, protect.
So let all fear and trembling cease—
The Lord will cover His elect.

O Lord, Please Answer When I Call
Based on Psalm 4

1. O Lord, please answer when I call! O God, my strength and righteousness, Your strength is great and mine is small— Give me relief from my distress!
2. How long, O men, will you corrupt My glory, turning it to shame? How long will you with lies erupt And serve the gods that have no name?
3. *Know that the* LORD *has set apart Unto Him self all godly men. So, trembling, cease! And doubt, depart! The* LORD *will hear my prayer. A men!*
4. *When you are angry, do not sin, But meditate upon your bed. Prepare your hearts and search within Before the of fered prayer is said.*
5. *While many scoff and many doubt And say, "Who shows us any good?" You fill us with more joy throughout Our lives than grain or new wine could.*
6. *I will lie down and sleep in peace, For You alone, O* LORD, *protect. So let all fear and trembling cease— The* LORD *will cover His elect.*

Music: Scottish hymn melody
Text: Douglas Wilson, 2022 ©

CAMERONIAN MIDNIGHT HYMN
8 8. 8 8.

PSALM 5

The Hatred of God

To the chief Musician upon Nehiloth, A Psalm of David.
Give ear to my words, O Lord,
consider my meditation.
Hearken unto the voice of my cry, my King, and my God:
for unto thee will I pray.
My voice shalt thou hear in the morning, O Lord;
in the morning will I direct my prayer unto thee, and will look up.
For thou art not a God that hath pleasure in wickedness:
neither shall evil dwell with thee.
The foolish shall not stand in thy sight:
thou hatest all workers of iniquity.
Thou shalt destroy them that speak leasing:

the Lord will abhor the bloody and deceitful man.
But as for me, I will come into thy house in the multitude of thy mercy:
and in thy fear will I worship toward thy holy temple.
Lead me, O Lord, in thy righteousness because of mine enemies;
make thy way straight before my face.
For there is no faithfulness in their mouth;
their inward part is very wickedness;
their throat is an open sepulchre;
they flatter with their tongue.
Destroy thou them, O God;
let them fall by their own counsels;
cast them out in the multitude of their transgressions;
for they have rebelled against thee.
But let all those that put their trust in thee rejoice:
let them ever shout for joy, because thou defendest them:
let them also that love thy name be joyful in thee.
For thou, Lord, wilt bless the righteous;
with favour wilt thou compass him as with a shield.

In this fifth psalm, we find the psalmist crying out to God for deliverance but also for more than deliverance. His desire is for God to vindicate His name and character as He destroys those who oppose His righteousness.

The psalm is given to the musician in charge of the wind instruments (*nehiloth*). The psalm is from David, and, once again, his trouble is great.

We begin with his prayer. David calls upon the Lord and asks Him to *hearken*. He asks God to consider and give ear (vv. 1–2). In offering the prayer, David is recognizing who God is (v. 2). He clearly understands the *Godness* of God.

This occurs in the morning—his thoughts turn to God when he awakes (v. 3). In the morning, David "assembles" his prayer. The word used here is the same as the word for arranging sacrifices on an altar, or showbread on the table. He looks *up*, like a guard on a watchtower, looking for a return message. The words of this prayer are his morning sacrifice.

David knows about the hatred of God. He begins with understatement—God has "no pleasure" in iniquity. Evil cannot live with Him (v. 4). Fools wither when He looks at them, and God hates those who work iniquity (v. 5). You read that right—God hates these men. Those who speak lies He will destroy, and He loathes bloody and deceitful men (v. 6).

But there is a contrast. David is not like these men. Surrounded by His mercy, and in the fear of God, David worships toward the temple (v. 7). He prays for God's righteous guidance and protection because of his enemies (v. 8). The men who oppose him, providing the contrast, are putrid and entirely corrupt (v. 9). Paul quotes this verse in Romans 3:13, applying it to all men everywhere. This is the natural condition of the human heart. David then pleads with God to take them out—*remove* them. The righteous cry out for God to display His righteous judgments. In particular, he prays that God would destroy them by their "own counsels" (v. 10).

There is still joy for those who love the Lord's name. In a world filled with warfare, those who trust in God can rejoice and shout for joy (v. 11). God is their defender; those who love His name can rejoice. God blesses the righteous and protects him with an encompassing buckler (v. 12).

All of this relates to worship as warfare. Let's return for a moment to what this passage says about God's hatred. God is holy, and He hates sin. And the only place where He distinguishes sin from the sinner in any way is in the cross. Outside of Christ, God never distinguishes the sin and sinner. It is not the *sin* He throws into the lake of fire.

We must remember what God does. He has "no pleasure" in some people (v. 4). He will not dwell with them (v. 4). His sight undoes the fool (v. 5), and He hates the worker of iniquity (v. 5). This is the same group that Jesus says will be told, "Depart from me, I never knew you" (Matt. 7:23). God will destroy liars (v. 6). He abhors bloody and deceitful men (v. 6).

But where do such individuals come from? The answer is that they grow up from little babies, and, in many cases, they were very cute babies. And even within the covenant, there was a *first* lie, a *first* deception, and it was a *little* thing. It was a little folly, it was a small iniquity. But it was a sin, so this is like saying it was a small enormity.

The devil has established a curriculum for fools. Our popular culture is a sewer pipe filled with the things condemned in this psalm. And a few words are offered to those young people who believe themselves mysteriously immune from such lies. They have taken the phrase *Christian worldview*, ground it to a fine dust, and sprinkled it over the tops of their heads. This keeps away the vampires of legalism. Thus protected with their Christian-worldview hooba dust, and *not* in the armor of Christ, they go out to the movies. They tell their mom that it is only rated OS–13—open sepulcher 13. They don't want to go *in*; they just want to sit outside and smell the stench. And *all* the cool kids are smelling the stench and catching flies. If you think like this, and more than a few young covenant members do, you are aspiring to be hated and loathed by

God. Lies surround us on every hand. Those who are enrolled in this curriculum of unbelief—playlists, video games, movies—then drop out.

One final word. The Bible tells us that we are engaged in a spiritual war, and that we do not wrestle against flesh and blood. The Lord Jesus Christ is our buckler, and He will destroy His enemies and ours. The great concern is that we not drift to the point where we find ourselves numbered among those enemies.

> Give ear, O Lord, to all my thoughts
> And words; now hear my crying.
> Please hear my voice, my King, my God,
> For unto Thee I offer
> My prayers at dawn, O Lord, you hear,
> You hear when night is dying.
> Hear my praying
> And know that I look up to Thee; my heart I proffer.
>
> For you are not a God who winks
> At evil in Your dwelling,
> And You can take no pleasure in
> The sins of evildoing.
> You hate those men who love their sin,
> Those men who lies are telling;
> You destroy them.
> The Lord abhors their bloody and deceitful choosing.

But as for me, I come to You,
And in Your house You found me.
And all Your mercies crowd me in;
I come in fear to tremble.
Lead me, O Lord, in righteousness;
My enemies surround me.
In Your presence
Make straight Your paths as we within Your house assemble.

Their mouths are foul, their inward parts
Are nothing but corruption.
Their throats are open tombs and graves;
They flatter with their speaking.
Destroy them, God, and bring them down
To end their vile seductions.
Hear my praying,
For they resist Your law; rebellion they are seeking.

But let those men who trust in You
Rejoice and sing forever
Because You are their shield and wall,
Their God and high defender.
No danger in the world can yet
From You Your loved ones sever.
Bless the righteous;
We joy in You alone and to Your love surrender.

Give ear, O Lord, to all my words,
Consider all my sighs.
Please listen to this cry for help;
To you my prayers will rise.

Dawn after dawn you hear my voice.
Dawn after dawn I kneel
And lay requests before your throne
And to your strength appeal.

With you the wicked cannot dwell;
You cannot stand their ways.
Before you proud men cannot come—
On them your anger stays.

You hate those men who live in wrong,
With them your justice wars.
All lying and bloodthirsty men
The holy Lord abhors.

But I will come into your house
And seek your mercy still.
In reverence will I bow down
Toward your holy hill.

Lead me, O Lord, in righteousness,
Make straight your holy way.
My enemies are all around—
Please keep their lies away.

PSALM 5: THE ROD OF IRON

Declare their guilt, O sovereign God,
I cannot trust their lies.
Their throats are open tombs and graves—
Please listen to my cries.

Give Ear, O Lord, to All My Thoughts
Based on Psalm 5

1. Give ear, O Lord, to all my thoughts And words; now hear my cry-ing.
2. For You are not a God who winks At e-vil in Your dwell-ing.
3. But as for me, I come to You, And in Your house You found me,
4. Their mouths are foul; their in-ward parts Are noth-ing but cor-rup-tion.
5. But let all those who trust in You Re-joice and sing for-ev-er

Please hear my voice, my King, my God, For un-to Thee I of-fer
And You can take no plea-sure in The sins of e-vil-do-ing.
And all Your mer-cies crowd me in; I come in fear to trem-ble.
Their throats are o-pen tombs and graves; They flat-ter with their speak-ing.
Be-cause You are their shield and wall, Their God and high de-fend-er.

My prayers at dawn, O Lord, You hear; You hear when night is dy-ing.
You hate those men who love their sin, Those men who lies are tell-ing;
Lead me, O Lord, in right-eous-ness; My en-e-mies sur-round me.
De-stroy them, God, and bring them down To end their vile se-duc-tions.
No dan-ger in the world can yet From You Your loved ones sev-er.

Hear my pray-ing And know that I look up to Thee; my heart I prof-fer.
You de-stroy them. The Lord ab-hors their blood-y and de-ceit-ful choos-ing.
In Your pre-sence Make straight Your paths as we with-in Your house as-sem-ble.
Hear my pray-ing, For they re-sist Your law; re-bel-lion they are seek-ing.
Bless the right-eous; We joy in You a-lone and to Your love sur-ren-der.

Music: Heinrich Schütz, 1661
Text: Douglas Wilson, 2000 ©

HERR, HÖR WAS ICH WILL [BECKER 5]
87. 87. 87. 4 6 7.

PSALM 6

Transactions of Grace

To the chief Musician on Neginoth upon Sheminith, A Psalm of David.
O Lord, rebuke me not in thine anger,
neither chasten me in thy hot displeasure.
Have mercy upon me, O Lord; for I am weak:
O Lord, heal me; for my bones are vexed.
My soul is also sore vexed:
but thou, O Lord, how long?
Return, O Lord, deliver my soul:
oh save me for thy mercies' sake.
For in death there is no remembrance of thee:
in the grave who shall give thee thanks?
I am weary with my groaning;

all the night make I my bed to swim;
I water my couch with my tears.
Mine eye is consumed because of grief;
it waxeth old because of all mine enemies.

Depart from me, all ye workers of iniquity;
for the Lord hath heard the voice of my weeping.
The Lord hath heard my supplication;
the Lord will receive my prayer.
Let all mine enemies be ashamed and sore vexed:
let them return and be ashamed suddenly.

We come now to one of many penitential psalms—psalms that grieve and sorrow over sin and cry for God to extend His mercy and grace.

Again, this is a psalm of David, although we are not given the occasion for it. This psalm is also for the strings, and it is to be "upon the eighth." This could refer to an eight-stringed harp, but another possibility is suggested by the literal translation "upon the octave."

The psalm begins with a prayer for restraint. David knows that he has sinned, and that he also merits punishment. At the same time, he prays that God would not discipline him according to his deserts. He does not want God to be heated or angry with him (v. 1). David's bones are vexed; he pleads with God on the basis of what he has already received and felt. He does not want God to assume that any more was needed (v. 2). He felt his weakness; his bones were vexed. In addition, his soul was vexed (v. 3). His prayer was a question—"God, how long do You think all this will remain necessary?" The answer is usually much longer than we want and much shorter than we fear.

Does God return? We know that God is omnipresent, and so in this sense, He cannot "return" anywhere. But to resort to metaphor, God can remove His blessing, and the psalmist assumes this and asks Him to return with that blessing. Any return would save him and would deliver his soul (v. 4).

David then deals with the silence of Sheol. David is still concerned with the glory of God (v. 5). Sheol was a land of forgetfulness, and who would render thanks to God from *there*? David does not overlook the final resurrection but still argues that nothing should diminish, even temporarily, thanksgiving to God.

The psalmist is wasted in his grief. He is weary with groaning; he floods his bed and couch with tears (v. 6). He has cried his eyes out (v. 7). He has been sick, he has sinned, and he must also deal with all his enemies.

Our God answers the prayers of sinners. The lament and prayer of David is answered while he is in the midst of offering his prayer. He is languishing under the hand of God, and then suddenly, in verse 8, his confidence returns. This confidence returns because God, as requested, has also returned. God will hear, David affirms (v. 9). A corollary to this is that his enemies will be abashed (v. 10). What was happening to David's bones will now happen to his adversaries.

Scripture teaches that sin flatters us at the beginning but wrecks us at the end. And godly discipline is no fun at the time, God says, but afterward it yields the peaceful fruit of an upright life (Heb. 12:11). This teaches us something interesting about pain and pleasure. Sin and righteousness *both* inflict pain, and they *both* bring pleasure. But when, where, and for how long? The pain brought by discipline can turn minutes into hours and hours into days. David cries out here—*How long?* But the pain brought to us by sin is everlasting.

In addition, the pleasures brought by sin are momentary. Moses preferred to suffer affliction with the people of God than to enjoy certain pleasures *for a season* (Heb. 11:25). But the pleasures of God? At His right hand are pleasures forevermore (Ps. 16:11).

The psalm also instructs us on the nature of truth and lies. We cannot enjoy being lied to without coming in a very short time to an enjoyment of lying. People who listen to lies about sin will soon be telling lies about sin. And here is the point: people who tell lies about sin don't like singing the psalms because it makes them tell the *truth* about sin.

Those who love the truth love to say it, sing it, talk about it, and hear it. And, fundamentally, they love to maintain the dividing wall between the truth and the lie. Repentance necessarily banishes those who work iniquity. Put another way, the Bible requires that you choose and maintain your friends wisely.

David knows that he needs forgiveness. He knows that if God were to chastise him to a full extent, it would destroy him. But he does not answer God in a resentful or angry way. He is humble, fully humble.

These transactions of grace are gibberish to the carnal mind. They make no sense because in a very important way, they are not transactions at all. The carnal mind cannot understand what it has never encountered.

O Lord, do not rebuke me
I cannot take Your wrath.
O Lord please show me mercy
I faint beneath Your hand.
My bones, Lord, are in agony;
I need Your healing touch.
My soul abides in anguish.
How long, O Lord, how much?

O Lord, turn and deliver,
Save with Your steadfast love.
A dead man is no giver—
Who praises from below?
I am worn out with groaning;
I flood my bed with tears.
My eyes are weak with sorrow—
They fail in all my fears.

Depart, you evildoers!
The Lord has heard my cry.
Depart, you evildoers,
The Lord accepts my prayer.
My foes will be disheartened;
My God will shame them here.
Disgraced, they will be routed
And shall retreat in fear.

O Lord, Do Not Rebuke Me

Based on Psalm 6

1. O Lord, do not rebuke me; I cannot take Your wrath.
   O Lord, please show me mercy; I faint beneath Your hand.
   My bones, Lord, are in agony; I need Your healing touch.
   My soul abides in anguish. How long, O Lord, how much?

2. O Lord, turn and deliver; Save with Your steadfast love.
   A dead man is no giver— Who praises from below?
   I am worn out with groaning; I flood my bed with tears.
   My eyes are weak with sorrow— They fail in all my fears.

3. Depart, you evildoers! The Lord has heard my cry.
   Depart, you evildoers, The Lord accepts my prayer.
   My foes will be disheartened; My God will shame them here.
   Disgraced, they will be routed And shall retreat in fear.

Music: Bartholomäus Gesius (1555–1613); harm. Johann Sebastian Bach (1674–1748)
Text: Douglas Wilson, 2015 ©

BEFIEHL DU DEINE WEGE
7 6. 7 6. 7 6. 7 6.

PSALM 7

No Level Playing Field

*Shiggaion of David, which he sang unto the Lord,
concerning the words of Cush the Benjamite.*
O Lord my God, in thee do I put my trust:
save me from all them that persecute me, and deliver me:
lest he tear my soul like a lion,
rending it in pieces, while there is none to deliver.
O Lord my God, if I have done this;
if there be iniquity in my hands;
if I have rewarded evil unto him that was at peace with me;
(yea, I have delivered him that without cause is mine enemy:)
let the enemy persecute my soul, and take it;
yea, let him tread down my life upon the earth,
and lay mine honour in the dust. Selah.

Arise, O Lord, in thine anger,
lift up thyself because of the rage of mine enemies:
and awake for me to the judgment that thou hast commanded.
So shall the congregation of the people compass thee about:
for their sakes therefore return thou on high.
The Lord shall judge the people:
judge me, O Lord, according to my righteousness,
and according to mine integrity that is in me.
Oh let the wickedness of the wicked come to an end;
but establish the just:
for the righteous God trieth the hearts and reins.

My defence is of God,
which saveth the upright in heart.
God judgeth the righteous,
and God is angry with the wicked every day.

If he turn not, he will whet his sword;
he hath bent his bow, and made it ready.
He hath also prepared for him the instruments of death;
he ordaineth his arrows against the persecutors.
Behold, he travaileth with iniquity,
and hath conceived mischief, and brought forth falsehood.
He made a pit, and digged it,
and is fallen into the ditch which he made.
His mischief shall return upon his own head,
and his violent dealing shall come down upon his own pate.

I will praise the Lord according to his righteousness:
and will sing praise to the name of the Lord most high.

The psalm is by David. The occasion of it was a slander by a particular man named Cush, a man from the same tribe that David's adversary Saul was from. The psalm is called a *shiggaion*, a "wandering," which probably refers to a very intense, dithyrambic poem (cf. Hab. 3:1).

In his zeal for vindication, David pours out his prayer passionately.

This wonderful psalm shows us that God will deliver us from lies as well as from other dangers. First, there is refuge in God. David needs deliverance from those who would persecute him (v. 1). Although there are many, one stands out in particular—Cush wants to tear David apart like a ravening lion (v. 2). If this were actually the case, there would be none to deliver, but David has taken refuge in God.

David also has the advantage of a clean conscience. When he turns to God, he can say with complete assurance that he is innocent. The way he does this is through calling for a curse to fall upon him if the charge is true (vv. 4–5). Not only is David innocent of the charge of iniquity in his hands (v. 3), not only is he not guilty of treachery (v. 4), he actually had once been the deliverer of his adversary (v. 4).

So this results in his cry to God. David prays to a delaying God, and asks Him to arise (v. 6). The congregation gathers to God, and David prays for their deliverance (v. 7). David is confident of an answer; he has prayed on the basis of his own righteousness and integrity (v. 8). This is a *comparative* righteousness, not an absolute one. He prays that wickedness would be destroyed, and he prays to the one who tries the hearts and reins (v. 9). This refers to the heart and kidneys—in the ancient world this metaphor referred to the seat of thought, affections, and passions. God is David's defense, and He is the one who saves the upright in heart (v. 10). We don't notice the reference to the heart because that is our idiom, while the kidneys strike us as being out of place. But the meaning is simply that he is speaking from the depths of his being.

What is the response of God? This prayer is not offered to one who is unwilling to act. God judges the righteous, and is angry with the wicked *constantly* (v. 11). If the slanderer does not repent, then God will deal with him (v. 12). God sharpens His sword; He steps on His bow in order to string it (v. 12). God builds the machinery of execution, and ordains His arrows to fly against the persecutors (v. 13). If God is the marksman, and the crosshairs are on your forehead, then what hope is there?

The wicked has slept with some foul thing, and has conceived mischief. He is now pregnant with evil, and is in labor to bring forth iniquity (v. 14). This plotting was a lot of work. He has dug a pit, which is labor intensive, and then has fallen into his own trap (v. 15). His own scheming will fall back down upon his own head (v. 16). God is not mocked; a man reaps what he sows. The only appropriate response to God for all His kindness is that of praise and thanksgiving (v. 17).

And this leads us to consider the sin of attempted neutrality. David is confident in this psalm that the slander against him was false. Because he was truly innocent, his charge against Cush was not an example of *him* slandering. Spiritual war is not a football game on a level playing field with the same rules applying to both sides.

Consider Jeremiah and Hananiah. When the famous battle of the prophets took place, who was right (Jer. 28:10)? Jeremiah said he was right. Hananiah said he was right.

Consider also the relationship between mercy and justice. God threw Pharaoh and his hosts into the Red Sea. Why? His mercy is forever (Ps. 136:15). He smote great kings. Why? Same reason (v. 17). He killed Og, the king of Bashan because His *mercy* is forever (v. 20).

And then there were the conflicts between Jesus and the Pharisees. Jesus said that the Pharisees were whited sepulchers full of dead men's bones and uncleanness. He spoke the sober truth (Matt. 23:27). When they said that He cast out demons by the prince of demons, they were guilty of blasphemy (Mark 3:29). Was it unfair that He was able to call them names when it was wicked for them to call Him names? Not at all. There is this concept called "the truth," with which moderns have no little trouble.

Beware of pseudohumility. The arrogance of man wants to pretend that lack of confidence in what God has revealed is humility and that confidence in what He has revealed is pride. This is a diabolical inversion. We are to be zealous for the true, the good, and the lovely, and the comeback in our relativistic age is always that we are zealous for such things as *we* understand them. And so and so over there disagrees, and respected scholars differ, and who are *you* to say that this is the truth of God?

Take care that you do not give anything away to the slanders of Cush. Do not, because of personal insecurities, trifle with the words of God.

O Lord my God, in You I trust,
Save me from those who hate.
Deliver me from lions' jaws,
And do not rise too late.

O Lord my God, if I have done
Deeds worthy of this end,
If I have been a treacherous man,
Or have betrayed a friend,

Then let him have his way with me,
And tread me into dust.
Yes, let him come and persecute,
And do what's only just.

Arise, O Lord, and show Your wrath;
My enemies all rage.
Awake for me, and judge them all,
And pay them with their wage.

So shall the people of the Lord
Encompass me in joy.
And for their sake, display Your strength
And thwart each evil ploy.

The Lord shall judge the people now:
Judge me, O Lord and God.
According to a righteous life,
My heart contains no fraud.

Oh, let my foes come to an end.
Make firm the just and right.
My righteous God tries hearts and reins,
And judges hateful spite.

So my defense is from the Lord,
    Who saves the just at heart.
God judges righteously and will
    Take up His saints' own part.

Unless He turns, His wrath will fall.
    He wields His bow and sword,
His arrows fly, and death descends;
    For them all wrath is stored.

The evildoers plan and plot,
    And so they bring forth lies.
They dig the pits they fall into,
    And all their mischief dies.

I praise the Lord, for He is just;
    His justice fills the sky.
I praise His high and holy name,
    The name of God Most High.

O Lord My God, in You I Trust

Based on Psalm 7:1–8

1. O Lord my God, in You I trust; Save me from those who hate.
2. O Lord my God, if I have done Deeds worthy of this end,
3. Then let him have his way with me And tread me into dust.
4. Arise, O Lord, and show Your wrath; My enemies all rage.
5. So shall the people of the Lord Encompass me in joy.
6. The Lord shall judge the people now: Judge me, O Lord and God.

Deliver me from lions' jaws, And do not rise too late.
If I have been a treach-'rous man, Or have betrayed a friend,
Yes, let him come and persecute And do what's only just.
Awake for me, and judge them all, And pay them with their wage.
And for their sake, display Your strength And thwart each evil ploy.
According to a righteous life— My heart contains no fraud.

Cont'd, Psalm 7:9–17

7. Oh, let my foes come to an end. Make firm the just and right.
8. So my defense is from the Lord Who saves the just at heart.
9. Unless He turns, His wrath will fall. He wields His bow and sword,
10. The evil-doers plan and plot, And so they bring forth lies.
11. I praise the Lord, for He is just; His justice fills the sky.

My righteous God tries hearts and reins, And judges hateful spite.
God judges righteously and will Take up His saints' own part.
His arrows fly, and death descends—For them all wrath is stored.
They dig the pits they fall into, And all their mischief dies.
I praise His high and holy name, The name of God Most High.

Music: Hugh Wilson (1766?–1824)
Text: Douglas Wilson, 2022 ©

MARTYRDOM
8 6. 8 6.

PSALM 8

Under His Feet

To the chief Musician upon Gittith, A Psalm of David.
O Lord our Lord, how excellent is thy name in all the earth!
who hast set thy glory above the heavens.

Out of the mouth of babes and sucklings
hast thou ordained strength because of thine enemies,
that thou mightest still the enemy and the avenger.
When I consider thy heavens, the work of thy fingers,
the moon and the stars, which thou hast ordained;
what is man, that thou art mindful of him?
and the son of man, that thou visitest him?
For thou hast made him a little lower than the angels,

and hast crowned him with glory and honour.
Thou madest him to have dominion over the works of thy hands;
thou hast put all things under his feet:
all sheep and oxen, yea, and the beasts of the field;
the fowl of the air, and the fish of the sea,
and whatsoever passeth through the paths of the seas.

O Lord our Lord, how excellent is thy name in all the earth!

The eighth psalm is another psalm of David. The import of the psalm is glorious, and the *Gittith* probably refers somehow to the joyful aspect and nature of the psalm.

We see first how the creation gives glory to God. The details of this psalm are sandwiched between two examples of high exultation (vv. 1, 9): God's name is excellent in all the earth, and His glory is above the heavens.

We should then note that victory is declared from the mouths of babes. Those who hate God and resist His will are defeated by Him. God defeats them in the words of *babies* (v. 2). Who shuts down the railing atheist? According to this psalm, the jabbering baby in the back of the sanctuary. *He* is the one who silences the foe and the avenger.

Of course, this relates to humility. When a man with a right heart considers the work of God's fingers in the heavens, he is abased and overwhelmed. Part of this is because God continues His kindnesses on our tiny level (vv. 3–4).

But despite a humble man's awareness that he is merely a piece of clay, God has nevertheless placed him just beneath in the angels in rank (v. 5) and has crowned him with glory and honor. The Lord Jesus came and occupied this place that was a little lower than the angels, and, in so doing, He exalted that place forever—in fact, in His ascension resulted in exalting it *above* the rank of the angels.

We therefore see true dominion: man is steward of the earth, and God has made him vicegerent over all beasts, birds, and fish (vv. 6–8).

We should carefully note the anchor points of this psalm. This psalm is frequently quoted in the New Testament, just as the second Psalm was, and we must use these quotations as anchor points in our interpretation of it. If we do not, then we will miss the point of the psalm entirely. One of the great tragedies in biblical commentary is how *infrequently* believing Christians take at face value the authoritative words of the New Testament on what a particular Old Testament passage means.

We have already commented on one of these places—"out of the mouths of babes." Jesus quotes the second verse of this psalm when certain self-important theologians were distressed over the behavior of children at Christ's triumphal entry of Jerusalem (Matt. 21:15–16). There is also a possible allusion to this psalm in Matt. 11:25. God has hidden these things from the wise and prudent, and revealed them to *babes*. Yet to this day, theologians continue to shoo babies away from Jesus.

And all things have been placed "under His feet." Whose feet? In the book of Hebrews, the apostle Paul applies this psalm *to mankind in Christ*. He is very clear about it.

> For unto the angels hath he not put in subjection the world to come, whereof we speak. But one in a certain place testified, say-

ing, What is man, that thou art mindful of him? or the son of man, that thou visitest him? Thou madest him a little lower than the angels; thou crownedst him with glory and honour, and didst set him over the works of thy hands: Thou hast put all things in subjection under his feet. For in that he put all in subjection under him, he left nothing that is not put under him. But now we see not yet all things put under him. But we see Jesus, who was made a little lower than the angels for the suffering of death, crowned with glory and honour; that he by the grace of God should taste death for every man. (Heb. 2:5–9)

We see the same thing in 1 Corinthians. Here Paul applies the psalm *to Christ*.

For he must reign, till he hath put all enemies under his feet. The last enemy that shall be destroyed is death. For he hath put all things under his feet. But when he saith all things are put under him, it is manifest that he is excepted, which did put all things under him. And when all things shall be subdued unto him, then shall the Son also himself be subject unto him that put all things under him, that God may be all in all. (1 Cor. 15:25–28)

Paul emphasizes this theme in Ephesians also. In Christ, mankind comes into his dominion.

Which he wrought in Christ, when he raised him from the dead, and set him at his own right hand in the heavenly places, far above all principality, and power, and might, and dominion, and every name that is named, not only in this world, but also in that which is to come: and hath put all things under his feet, and gave him to be the head over all things to the church, which is his body, the fulness of him that filleth all in all. (Eph. 1:20–23)

Mankind is in the process of growing up to his maturity in Christ. But in recent times, our difficulty in understanding covenantal identity has really crippled us. Jesus Christ is not the isolated perfect man. Jesus Christ is the new mankind, He is the new Adam, He is the new race of man. And all who are in Him are included in this glorious new dominion.

The ruin created by the first Adam is being repaired in the person and work of the second Adam. We are invited to see the restoration of the entire earth in Christ—and if we are more dependent on our newspapers than on the Word of God, the author of Hebrews both encourages and admonishes us. We do not *yet* see everything subject to mankind in Christ, but we *do* see Jesus Christ, and to the extent we see Him by faith, in line with what the New Testament teaches about this, the world will be subdued under the preaching of the gospel.

Everything has been placed under the feet of Jesus Christ. But we are His body; *we* are His feet.

> Lord, our Lord, Your name is glorious,
> And Your name is great on earth!
> Over skies You set Your glory;
> Heavens all proclaim Your worth.
> From the mouths of babes and sucklings
> You ordained great strength to come.

I consider all Your heavens,
And the works Your fingers made—
Moon and stars, all in their courses.
What is man, with grace his aid?
What is man that You would visit?
What is man that You should care?

You have made him slightly lower
Than the angels and sent down
Glory, honor, and dominion
For his legacy and crown.
You have put creation under
Mankind's feet in Christ alone.

Sheep and oxen and wild creatures,
Birds in flight and meadow beasts,
All the fish that swim through waters,
Of them all we now are priests.
Lord, our Lord, Your name is glorious,
And your name is great on earth!

Lord Our Lord, Your Name Is Glorious
Based on Psalm 8

1. Lord, our Lord, Your name is glorious, And Your name is great on earth!
   O-ver skies You set Your glory; Heav-ens all proclaim Your worth.
2. I consider all Your heavens And the works Your fingers made—
   Moon and stars, all in their courses. What is man with grace his aid?
3. You have made him slightly lower Than the angels and sent down
   Glory, honor, and dominion For his legacy and crown.
4. Sheep and oxen and wild creatures, Birds in flight and meadow beasts,
   All the fish that swim through waters, Of them all we now are priests.

From the mouths of babes and sucklings You ordained great strength to come.
What is man that You would visit? What is man that You should care?
You have put creation under Mankind's feet in Christ alone.
Lord, our Lord, Your name is glorious, And Your name is great on earth!

Music: Michael E. Owens, 2022
Text: Douglas Wilson, 2022 ©

FORESHADOW
87.87.87.

PSALM 9

Poetic Justice

To the chief Musician upon Muth-labben, A Psalm of David.
I will praise thee, O Lord, with my whole heart;
I will shew forth all thy marvellous works.
I will be glad and rejoice in thee:
I will sing praise to thy name, O thou most High.

When mine enemies are turned back,
they shall fall and perish at thy presence.
For thou hast maintained my right and my cause;
thou satest in the throne judging right.
Thou hast rebuked the heathen,
thou hast destroyed the wicked,

thou hast put out their name for ever and ever.
O thou enemy, destructions are come to a perpetual end:
and thou hast destroyed cities;
their memorial is perished with them.

But the Lord shall endure for ever:
he hath prepared his throne for judgment.
And he shall judge the world in righteousness,
he shall minister judgment to the people in uprightness.
The Lord also will be a refuge for the oppressed,
a refuge in times of trouble.
And they that know thy name will put their trust in thee:
for thou, Lord, hast not forsaken them that seek thee.

Sing praises to the Lord, which dwelleth in Zion:
declare among the people his doings.
When he maketh inquisition for blood, he remembereth them:
he forgetteth not the cry of the humble.
Have mercy upon me, O Lord;
consider my trouble which I suffer of them that hate me,
thou that liftest me up from the gates of death:
that I may shew forth all thy praise in the gates of the daughter of
Zion:
I will rejoice in thy salvation.

The heathen are sunk down in the pit that they made:
in the net which they hid is their own foot taken.
The Lord is known by the judgment which he executeth:
the wicked is snared in the work of his own hands.
Higgaion. Selah.

> The wicked shall be turned into hell,
> and all the nations that forget God.
> For the needy shall not alway be forgotten:
> the expectation of the poor shall not perish for ever.
>
> Arise, O Lord; let not man prevail:
> let the heathen be judged in thy sight.
> Put them in fear, O Lord:
> that the nations may know themselves to be but men.
> Selah.

---

*I*n this psalm, David recounts his fight with the heathen who had invaded his nation. David writes during the course of a brief respite in the battle. He celebrates a great deliverance in the first part of the psalm (vv. 1–12) and calls for further deliverance in the remainder of the psalm (vv. 13–20).

Incidentally, this is the point where the numbering of the psalms becomes confused because some ancient versions include the tenth psalm as the second part of this psalm. The meaning of *muthlabben* is obscure.

First, we see the deliverance past. Praise is fitting; the one who chooses to recount the deeds of the Lord will never have a shortage of things to talk about (vv. 1–2). This is to be done with a *whole* heart. We are to praise the name of the *most High* God.

The presence of the Lord is important in battle. David's enemies are turned back, but not through *his* prowess. They are undone by the presence of the Lord (v. 3). God has not sided with David arbitrarily—He decided for David, but did so sitting on the throne, judging rightly (v. 4).

And so it is that the destroyers are destroyed. God has destroyed the wicked and has obliterated their name forever (v. 5). These were the ones who had sought to make a name for themselves by destroying cities. But *their* destructions are ended (v. 6). In contrast, the Lord will endure forever, and His judgments will stand (v. 7).

Those judgments which stand are *upright* judgments. In his address at Mars Hill, Paul quotes the Septuagint version of this verse (v. 8, cf. Acts 17:31). Jesus Christ is the culmination of this most glorious process of defeating the wicked. God will judge the world and will minister justice, and God has given proof of this by raising Jesus from the dead, thereby establishing Him as the judge of all nations.

God is a refuge. He is a refuge for the oppressed (v. 9), for all those in trouble. Those who know His name will turn to Him, and He will not forsake them (v. 10). Again, He is worthy of all praise for His *doings* (v. 11). God *acts* in history.

Because He acts in history, He conducts an inquisition. God will carefully search out all unlawful shedding of blood. Those whose blood has been shed, and whose cry has gone up to heaven, will be therefore vindicated (v. 12).

But deliverance is still necessary in the future. David has seen God work a great deliverance, but he is still in trouble.

And so he asks, "Have mercy on me, O Lord." He asks God to deliver him from those who hate him and who want to kill him (v. 13). His motive in asking this is so that he might glorify God's name (v. 14). He asks to be removed from the gates of death so that he can praise God in the gates of the daughter of Zion.

The heathen are therefore sunk. God is not mocked. The heathen have dug their own pit, they have set their own trap, and they are caught in it (v. 15). God hangs all envious Hamans on their own gallows. This is how God works (v. 16). *Think* about this. *Higgaion* and *Selah*. This is one of the ways God makes himself known in history—when treacherous scoundrels fall into their own traps.

What happens to those who forget God? The wicked are turned into Sheol. This is what happens to all nations that forget God (v. 17) because God does not leave the poor forgotten (v. 18).

"Arise, O Lord." The prayer is for men to not prevail, and for the heathen to be judged in the sight of the Lord (v. 19). Because they are *sorry* little men, the psalmist asks God to put them all in fear, so that they will know that they are only men (v. 20).

In all this, several key applications should immediately occur to us.

First, we need to recognize the sin of forgetfulness. Forgetting is not an excuse for having sinned; it is another sin in its own right. The people who forget God are a people who are turned into judgment, and ultimately, into Hell.

Second, poetic justice is a biblical category, and not just a plot device for ham-handed novelists. God does not merely render justice; He does so *fittingly*. The fool thinks that the "breaks" are a matter of random chance and yet that they always somehow go against him. But God governs the world through blessings and curses. We do not absolutize this—remember both Job and the man born blind—but we do still believe it.

And third, what is man? The question can be asked in two different ways. We can ask it in the way David does in the previous psalm—referring to *man under grace*. But the question can be asked another way: when we are talking about *man under judgment*. When we consider how man is not much, we must marvel either at God's kindness or at man's insolence.

Lord, I will praise You with my whole heart;
I will set forth Your deeds and works.
I will be glad and stand rejoicing
To sing Your praises, God Most High.

When all my foes are turned in panic,
They shall fall down before Your face.
For You took up my cause, defending,
And sat enthroned to judge the right.

The heathen You rebuked in anger,
And You destroyed them utterly.
You blotted out their name forever
And caused their fame to die and rot.

For now, my foe, your failed destructions
Have come here to their final end.
Defeated cities, no memorial,
But God shall ever live and reign.

Our God prepared his throne for judgment.
He judges earth in righteousness.
He brings true judgment to the people.
The Lord Himself will be their fort.

And those who know Your name as holy
Will put their faith and trust in You,

For You, O Lord, do not forsake us,
You always keep your children safe.

Sing praise to God who dwells in Zion.
Declare to all His mighty works.
When shed blood calls for inquisition,
Our God will hear our humble cries.

O Lord my God, bring mercy to me;
Consider all my troubles now
Beneath the hands of those who hate me,
And lift me to the gates of life.

So I will now possess salvation.
The heathen fell into a pit—
They spread their net, and they were taken.
The Lord snared them with His own hands.

The wicked shall come to destruction,
And all the nations that forget.
The needy shall not be forgotten:
Arise, O Lord; put man in fear.

Lord, I Will Praise You with My Whole Heart

Based on Psalm 9:1–9

1. ₁Lord, I will praise You with my whole heart; I will set forth Your deeds and works. ₂I will be glad and stand rejoicing To sing Your praises, God Most High.
2. ₃When all my foes are turned in panic, They shall fall down before Your face. ₄For You took up my cause, defending, And sat enthroned to judge the right.
3. ₅*The heathen You rebuked in anger, And You destroyed them utterly. You blotted out their name forever And caused their fame to die and rot.*
4. ₆For now, my foe, your failed destructions Have come here to their final end. Defeated cities, no memorial, ₇But God shall ever live and reign.
5. Our God prepared His throne for judgment. ₈He judges earth in righteousness. He brings true judgment to the people. ₉The Lord Himself will be their fort.

Cont'd, Psalm 9:10–20

6. 10And those who know Your name as holy Will put their faith and trust in You, For You, O Lord, do not forsake us, You always keep Your children safe.
7. 11Sing praise to GOD who dwells in Zion. Declare to all His mighty works. 12When shed blood calls for iniquity, Our God will hear our humble cries.
8. 13*O LORD my God, bring mercy to me; Consider all my troubles now Beneath the hands of those who hate me, And lift me to the gates of life.*
9. 14So I will now possess salvation. 15The heathen fell into a pit— They spread their net, and they are taken. 16The LORD ensnared them with His hands.
10. 17The wicked shall come to destruction, And all the nations that forget. 18The needy shall not be forgotten: 19Arise, O LORD; 20put man in fear.

Music: Felix Mendelssohn-Bartholdy (1809–1847)
Text: Douglas Wilson, 2022 ©

SELWYN
9 8. 9 8.

PSALM 10

Break Their Evil Arms

Why standest thou afar off, O Lord?
why hidest thou thyself in times of trouble?
The wicked in his pride doth persecute the poor:
let them be taken in the devices that they have imagined.
For the wicked boasteth of his heart's desire,
and blesseth the covetous, whom the Lord abhorreth.
The wicked, through the pride of his countenance, will not seek
after God:
God is not in all his thoughts.
His ways are always grievous;
thy judgments are far above out of his sight:
as for all his enemies, he puffeth at them.

He hath said in his heart, I shall not be moved:
for I shall never be in adversity.
His mouth is full of cursing and deceit and fraud:
under his tongue is mischief and vanity.
He sitteth in the lurking places of the villages:
in the secret places doth he murder the innocent:
his eyes are privily set against the poor.
He lieth in wait secretly as a lion in his den:
he lieth in wait to catch the poor:
he doth catch the poor, when he draweth him into his net.
He croucheth, and humbleth himself,
that the poor may fall by his strong ones.
He hath said in his heart, God hath forgotten:
he hideth his face; he will never see it.

Arise, O Lord; O God, lift up thine hand:
forget not the humble.
Wherefore doth the wicked contemn God?
he hath said in his heart, Thou wilt not require it.
Thou hast seen it;
for thou beholdest mischief and spite, to requite it with thy hand:
the poor committeth himself unto thee;
thou art the helper of the fatherless.
Break thou the arm of the wicked and the evil man:
seek out his wickedness till thou find none.
The Lord is King for ever and ever:
the heathen are perished out of his land.
Lord, thou hast heard the desire of the humble:
thou wilt prepare their heart,
thou wilt cause thine ear to hear:

> to judge the fatherless and the oppressed,
> that the man of the earth may no more oppress.

---

*A*s with so many of the psalms, this psalm shows one of God's saints in great turmoil over the condition of the fat and sassy attitude of those who rebel against heaven. In a world where sin is a horrible reality, God's people are to learn *how to pray against it*. This prayer is just such an example of how we are to pray. We see first the virtues of holy complaint: from the vantage point of the saints, it sometimes looks as though God is standing off somewhere else. And so this sanctified complaint drives the prayer (v. 1).

In the second verse, we come to a statement of the problem—the wicked in their conceit are assaulting the poor—along with the pious wish that the wicked would be caught in their own snares (v. 2).

We see then how the wicked think. The actions of the wicked are the fruit of their heart condition—this is how they think in their hearts. God hates the covetous, but the wicked *bless* the covetous (v. 3) as well as boasting in their own lusts and desires. The wicked resist God on the outside of their heads and on the inside. God is excluded through pride of countenance, and God is not in their thoughts (v. 4). The wicked man's thoughts are earthbound (v. 5), and he puffs at his enemies. In all things, he is bulletproof (v. 6).

We then return to what the wicked *do*. The wicked are sneaking, malicious thieves (v. 7) with vain talk under their tongues. Such a man lurks in order to waylay the innocent and defenseless (vv. 8–9). He abuses his own dignity in order to destroy the poor (v. 10).

We come back again to how the wicked think. They deceive themselves and believe that God does not see this (v. 11).

And so this is the holy complaint and prayer. The psalmist beseeches God to arise and do something. The wicked say God has forgotten, and the godly beg Him *not* to forget (v. 12). They do not share a common premise here—that God can forget the humble—rather, the division between them is ethical. Listen to what the wicked say! They say that God does not judge sin (v. 13). But the psalmist knows that God has in fact seen it, and that He will requite it (v. 14). God the Father is the God of the fatherless. And the fatherless may cry out to Him and ask Him to come down and break the arms of the wicked (v. 15).

The psalm concludes with deliverance. God is king forever; the heathen are dead (v. 16). God has heard the prayers of the humble (v. 17). He prepares the heart of the humble to pray, and He causes His own ear to hear (v. 17).

What are some basic applications for us? This psalm is by no means a devotional fossil. It is as relevant today as the day it was first written.

"Arise, O Lord." In the first and twelfth verses, the psalmist begs God to *do something*. If our Reformed theology keeps us from praying this way, then our Reformed theology needs some adjusting.

God sees. A heretical movement today within the larger evangelical world wants to say that God does not know everything, and that everything is in process and flux. But whenever a *sinner* maintains that God does not know all things, it is because he does not *want* God to know everything. That is, there is something he wants to hide, and that something is always sin. This is what we see in verse 11.

God prepares for reformation. Notice how God hears the desire of the humble (v. 17). He prepares their hearts, and also He causes His own ear to hear. This means, for example, that our prayers for the reformation of the church are prayers that God has given to us in the first place. He has placed this desire within us, and we can be confident that He is also causing His ear to hear us. God does not create the thirst without creating the water.

We learn here the importance of breaking some arms. Are there no arms today which need breaking? Is there no insolence in our halls of justice? Are there no enthroned criminals who make life wretched for the humble of the earth? Is it not true that our authorities refuse to heed what God has told them to do? And should we not make the great application of praying this way? Come down, our Lord and God, and break their evil arms. We may pray that God would start with the Supreme Court, and then move on to the various circuit courts. Then on to Congress! To refuse to pray in this way is not so much to deny the evil as it is in some fashion to join it.

> Why do you stand far off, O God, my LORD,
> And why in times of trouble do You hide?
> The wicked in their hate cannot afford
> To spare the poor from persecuting pride.
> Let them be caught as all their schemes collide.
> He boasts of lust which from his heart arises;
> He blesses greedy men whom God despises.
>
> The wicked gloat, and in their pride of face
> Will not seek after God or think of Him.
> Their ways are always grievous to His grace;
> His judgments to their eyes are blurred and dim,

They scoff at coming dangers, fell and grim,
As in their hearts they say they can't be shaken,
And claim they cannot be in troubles taken.

Their mouths are full of cursing and deceit,
And under their vain tongues is mischief wrought.
Their words seek ways to lure, defraud, and cheat;
They lurked in alleys and from hiding sought
The blood of innocents; the poor are caught.
They lie in wait; their nets are laid down slowly;
They set their traps; they scheme to catch the lowly.

They crouch beside their traps and are disgraced.
They wait to catch the poor by their own hand
And say within their hearts, "God hides His face;
He has forgotten us. Our schemes will stand,
For God will never see what we have planned."
Arise, our Lord and God, bring Your salvation
And save the humble from humiliation.

Why do the wicked thus condemn the Lord?
Why do they think He will not judge their sin?
Our God has seen it all and lifts His sword;
God marks the mischief and the spite within
Their evil hearts—His judgments soon begin.
O God, the wicked scorn all true repentance.
The fatherless rely upon Your sentence.

O God, come down and break their evil arms.
Seek out their sins and chase them all away.

The Lord is King, and, freed from all alarms,
We rest in Him. The heathen fade away.
O Lord, You always hear the humble pray
As You prepare their hearts for Your own blessing.
You hear their cry and judge all vain oppressing.

Why Do You Stand Far Off, O God My Lord?
Based on Psalm 10

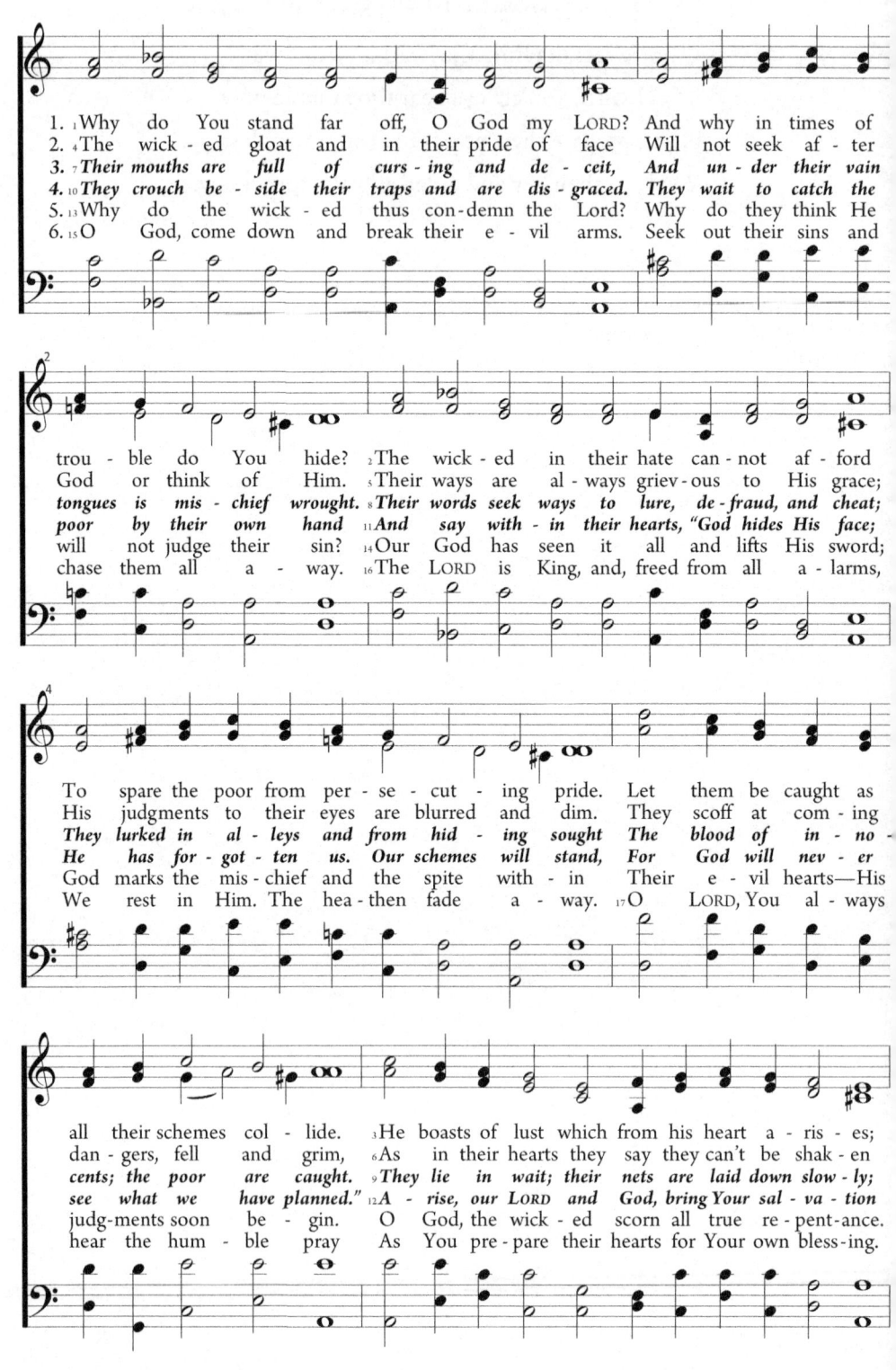

1. ₁Why do You stand far off, O God my Lord? And why in times of trouble do You hide? ₂The wicked in their hate cannot afford To spare the poor from persecuting pride. Let them be caught as all their schemes collide. ₃He boasts of lust which from his heart arises;

2. ₄The wicked gloat and in their pride of face Will not seek after God or think of Him. ₅Their ways are always grievous to His grace; His judgments to their eyes are blurred and dim. They scoff at coming dangers, fell and grim, ₆As in their hearts they say they can't be shaken

3. ₇Their mouths are full of cursing and deceit, And under their vain tongues is mischief wrought. ₈Their words seek ways to lure, defraud, and cheat; They lurked in alleys and from hiding sought The blood of innocents; the poor are caught. ₉They lie in wait; their nets are laid down slowly;

4. ₁₀They crouch beside their traps and are disgraced. They wait to catch the poor by their own hand ₁₁And say within their hearts, "God hides His face; He has forgotten us. Our schemes will stand, For God will never see what we have planned." ₁₂Arise, our Lord and God, bring Your salvation

5. ₁₃Why do the wicked thus condemn the Lord? Why do they think He will not judge their sin? ₁₄Our God has seen it all and lifts His sword; God marks the mischief and the spite within Their evil hearts—His judgments soon begin. O God, the wicked scorn all true repentance.

6. ₁₅O God, come down and break their evil arms. Seek out their sins and chase them all away. ₁₆The Lord is King, and, freed from all alarms, We rest in Him. The heathen fade away. ₁₇O Lord, You always hear the humble pray As You prepare their hearts for Your own blessing.

He	bless - es	greed - y	men	whom	God	de - spis		-	es.
And	claim they	can - not	be	in	trou - bles	tak		-	en.
They	*set their*	*traps; they*	*scheme*	*to*	*catch*	*the*	*low*	*-*	*ly.*
And	*save the*	*hum - ble*	*from*	*hu -*	*mil -*	*i -*	*a*	*-*	*tion.*
The	fa - ther - less	re - ly	up - on	Your	sen		-	tence.
₁₈You	hear their	cry and	judge	all	vain	op - press		-	ing.

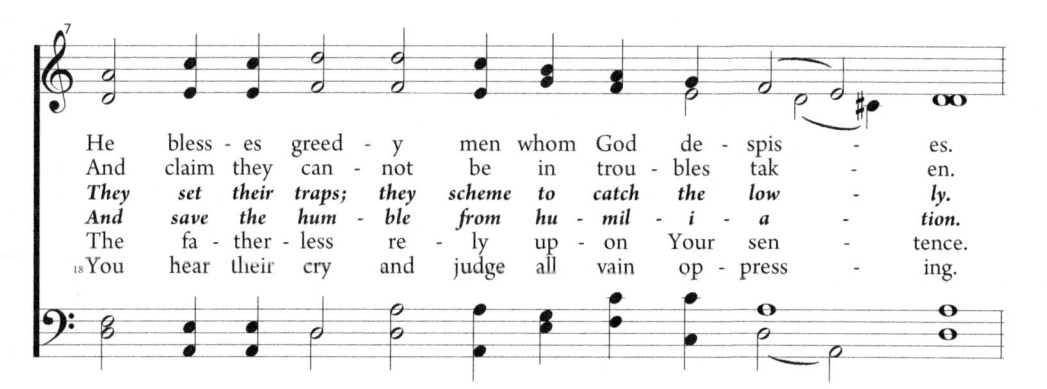

Music: Genevan Psalter, 1542; harm. Claude Goudimel, 1564
Text: Douglas Wilson, 2000 ©

D'OÙ VIENT CELA, SEIGNEUR [GENEVAN 10
10 10. 10 10. 10 11 11

Printed in Great Britain
by Amazon